SEE: Adventures at Prosperity Patch

by Kim D. H. Butler
and Spencer Shaw

SEE: Adventures at Prosperity Patch
Copyright © 2025 Kim D. H. Butler and Spencer Shaw

Prosperity Economics Movement
22790 Highway 259 South
Mount Enterprise, TX 75681
www.ProsperityEconomics.org

First Edition
ISBN: 979-8-9940994-0-7 (paperback)

Produced in the United States of America

Published with the assistance of Social Motion Publishing, which specializes in books that benefit causes and nonprofits. For more information, go to SocialMotionPublishing.com.

DISCLAIMER: Although the author and publisher have made every effort to ensure that the information in this book was correct at press time, the author and publisher do not assume and hereby disclaim any liability to any party for any loss, damage, or disruption caused by errors or omissions, whether such errors or omissions result from negligence, accident, or any other cause. This book is also not intended to provide specific financial or legal advice. The author and publisher do not assume and hereby disclaim any liability to any party for any loss, damage, or disruption caused by the information in this book. For advice and guidance specific to your situation, please contact the Prosperity Economics Movement or a qualified expert. If you do not agree to these terms, you may return this book to the Prosperity Economics Movement for a full refund.

TRADEMARK NOTICE: Prosperity Economic, Prosperity Economics, Prosperity Economic Advisor, Prosperity Economic Advisors, and Prosperity Ladder are trademarks of Prosperity Economics Movement.

Acknowledgments

I love animals; I have had dogs, cats, chickens, pigs, sheep, goats, and dairy cows since 4th grade, and now I have Alpacas! I also love Prosperity Thinking. Now, I am excited to share these loves with children of all ages through my third love: reading! Whether you are an adult or have children, grandchildren, or great-grandchildren, reading with others (and playing games too!) is a fabulous bonding experience, and I am so grateful to the team of Spencer and family for bringing it to your table.

Enjoy, Kim Butler, Mount Enterprise, TX

I grew up hearing stories from my dad and kinfolk which shaped my world today. Sharing stories with kids is a fun way to help them think about big dreams. Huge thank you to my wife for leading our homeschooling and our kids for listening to these stories. A big thank you to Emma for helping Kim and I feel like children again.

We are so grateful to everyone who helps us make this book, like Amanda who leads this project and our awesome designers Cy and Holly.

Spencer Shaw

Prosperity Patch was buzzing with energy, as everyone was getting ready for the grand Harvest Festival. The farm, a hub of joy and learning, was glowing with the beautiful colors of autumn. Emma, the wise Great Dane, was in charge of preparations, her observant eyes missing nothing.

While her friends dove into their tasks with excitement, Emma couldn't help but notice that something was out of balance which could mean chaos for the festival. With each pet absorbed in their own world, the big event they all cherished was shaping up to be a bit disorganized.

Zippy the Rabbit, the one with the most energy, was tangled up in streamers and fairy lights, his area looking more like a disaster than a festival.

Nearby, Peanut the Cat was inventing a treasure hunt game, oblivious to how it interfered with the food stalls. Miguel the Bull was setting up with his usual precision, but very much in the way of others.

With just two days to go, Emma gathered her friends under the shade of a large oak. "Friends," Emma started, her voice as calm as the gentle stream nearby, "we all want this festival to be a wonderful one. But we're missing the grand scheme of things."

She spread out a detailed map of Prosperity Patch on an old picnic table.

"Look here," Emma continued, pointing to the layout. "Zippy, your decorations are awesome, but they need to guide visitors, not just dazzle them. And Peanut, your game could be a hit, but let's move it to the open field where it won't clash with Miguel's food stalls."

The pets leaned in, studying the map. Slowly, the big picture Emma was explaining came into focus. Realizing this, they agreed to rearrange their tasks to better help each other, allowing a good flow for the festival.

Over the next two days, Prosperity Patch transformed.

Zippy's decorations now lined pathways, leading visitors through the farm.

Peanut's treasure hunt became the festival's highlight, positioned away from the hustle and bustle yet easy to find.

Miguel's stalls were placed to catch the flow of traffic, his fresh produce and treats tempting guests as they moved from one attraction to the next.

When the festival day arrived, the sun shone brightly, casting a warm glow over a perfect scene.

Guests moved smoothly from one part of the festival to another, their laughter and chatter filling the air with energy.

The pets watched with pride as their hard work paid off, the festival was a big success!

As the day drew to a close, Emma and her friends gathered once again under the oak tree.

"Today, we saw how important it is to step back and see how everything connects," Emma reflected. "By not getting wrapped up in our own projects and seeing how it can all flow in harmony, we achieved something great together."

Emma's Advice:

Hello, young planners! When you're getting ready to organize an event or outing, it's super helpful to have a "big picture" mindset. Imagine you're putting together a big puzzle. Each piece is important, like choosing the right games, snacks, or making sure everyone knows the plan. By thinking about how all the pieces fit, you can make sure nothing is forgotten and everyone has a great time. Remember, planning is like an adventure, and with your creativity and teamwork, you can make it extra special!

Emma's Questions:

- Why is it important to see how different parts of a story or puzzle fit together?

- Can you remember a time when seeing the whole picture helped you understand something better?
- How do you feel when you only look at a small part of something? Does it make it harder to understand?
- How can looking at the whole picture help you make good choices each day?

A note for your parents!

As our thank-you, the QR code below will give you a valuable white paper focused on Income Strategies at ProsperityEconomics.org/permission.

www.ingramcontent.com/pod-product-compliance
Lightning Source LLC
Chambersburg PA
CBHW042218050426
42453CB00001BA/13